FOX SEARCHLIGHT PICTURES WARNER BROS. PICTURES CELADOR FILMS FILM4 PRESENT A CELADOR FILMS PRODUCTION A DANNY BOYLE FILM "SLUMDOG MILLIONAIRE"
DEV PATEL FREIDA PINTO MADHUR MITTAL ANIL KAPOOR IRRFAN KAHN CASTING BY LOVELEEN TANDAN GAIL STEVENS CDG MAKE UP & HAIR DESIGN NATASHA NISCHOL & VIRGINIA HOLMES
SOUND MIXER RESUL POOKUTTY SOUND DESIGNER GLENN FREEMANTLE COSTUME DESIGNER SUTTIRAT ANNE LARLARB MUSIC COMPOSED AND PRODUCED BY A. R. RAHMAN CO-EXECUTIVE PRODUCERS FRANÇOIS IVERNEL CAMERON McCRACKEN LINE PRODUCER TABREZ NOORANI
CO-PRODUCER PAUL RITCHIE EDITOR CHRIS DICKENS PRODUCTION DESIGNER MARK DIGBY DIRECTOR OF PHOTOGRAPHY ANTHONY DOD MANTLE BSC DFF EXECUTIVE PRODUCERS PAUL SMITH TESSA ROSS BASED ON THE NOVEL "Q&A" BY VIKAS SWARUP PRODUCED BY CHRISTIAN COLSON
SCREENPLAY BY SIMON BEAUFOY CO-DIRECTOR (INDIA) LOVELEEN TANDAN DIRECTED BY DANNY BOYLE

www.foxsearchlight.com

ISBN 978-1-4234-7950-5

HAL•LEONARD® CORPORATION
7777 W. BLUEMOUND RD. P.O. BOX 13819 MILWAUKEE, WI 53213

Visit Hal Leonard Online at
www.halleonard.com

O, SAYA

Words and Music by MATHANGI ARULPRAGASAM
and A R RAHMAN

Moderately fast

Ah ____ ro - ha _____ ma - zo _____

ma - yo _____ hey ____ ah _____

yo. ____ Ay - a ri - ha ra - ya o - ra - zhi - a,

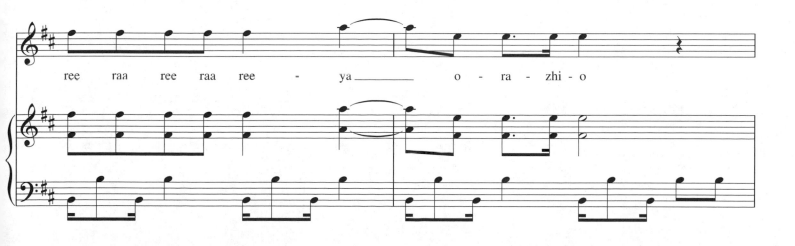

ree raa ree raa ree - ya _____ o - ra - zhi - o

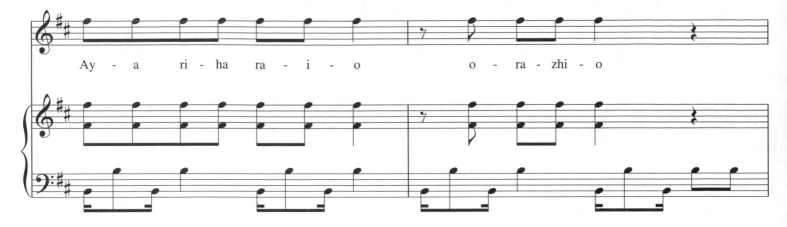

ro - ha _____ ma - yo. _____ Ay

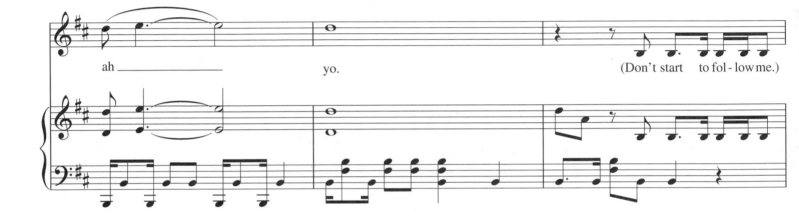

ah _____ yo. (Don't start to fol-low me.)

Ay - a ri - ha ra - ya o - ra - zhi - a,
(To hang in a bar.) (Wan - na be a star.)

ree raa ree raa ree - ya _____ o - ra - zhi - o
(Pick up the pack for my jour - ney.)

O, sa - ya _____

F#7#5

ye - ro. _____ (Don't start to fol - low me.)

Em9

O, sa - ya _____

G   Cmaj9#11

ye - ro _____ ma - yo.
(Ek do teen char panch che saath aat nao das gya - ra ba - ra te - raa.)

MAUSAM & ESCAPE

Music and Lyrics by
A R RAHMAN

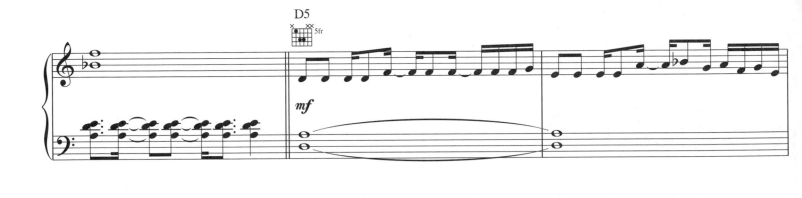

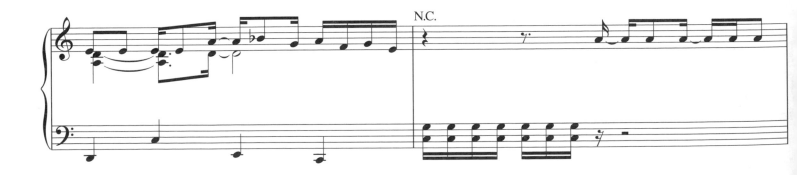

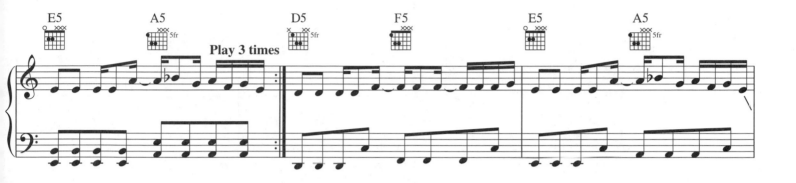

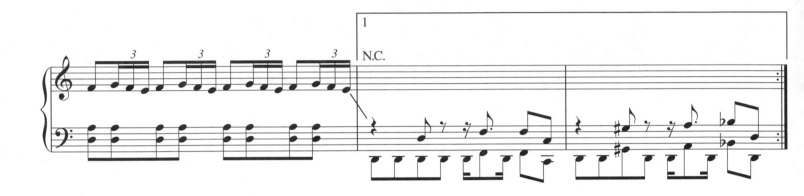

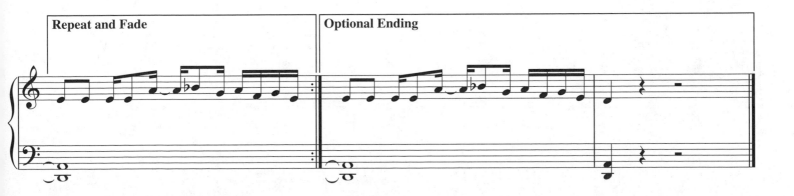

PAPER PLANES

Words and Music by JOE STRUMMER,
MICK JONES, PAUL SIMONON,
TOPPER HEADON, THOMAS PENTZ
and MATHANGI ARULPRAGASAM

fly like pa - per, get high like planes. If you catch me at the bor - der, I got vi - sas in my name. If you
Pi - rate skulls and bones. Sticks and stones and weed and bombs.

come a - round here, I make 'em all day. I get one done in a sec - ond if you wait. I
Run - ning when we hit 'em. Le - thal poi - son through their sys - tem.

Some-times I think sit-ting on trains. Ev-'ry stop I get to, I'm clock-ing that game.
No one on the cor-ner has swag-ger like us. Hit me on my burn-er pre-paid wire-less. We

Ev-'ry-one's a win-ner, we're mak-ing our fame, bo-na fide hus-tl-er mak-ing my name.
pack and de-liv-er like U. P. S. trucks, al-read-y go-ing hell, just pump-ing that gas.

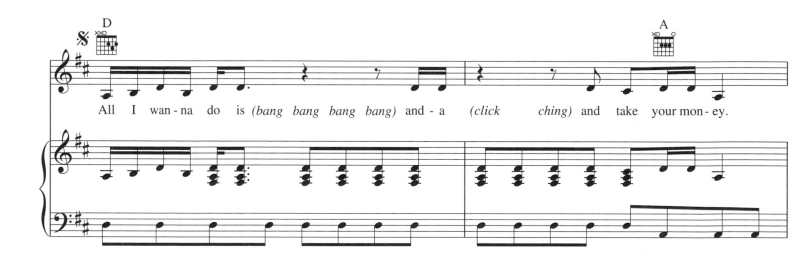

All I wan-na do is (bang bang bang bang) and-a (click ching) and take your mon-ey.

All I wan-na do is (bang bang bang bang) and-a (click ching) and take your mon-ey.

All I wan-na do is *(bang bang bang bang)* and - a *(click ching)* and take your mon - ey.

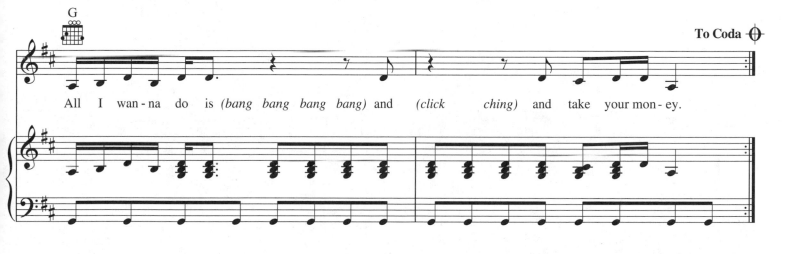

To Coda ⊕

All I wan-na do is *(bang bang bang bang)* and *(click ching)* and take your mon - ey.

(Spoken:) M.I.A., third world democracy, yeah, I've got more records than the K.G.B,

so, ah, no funny business.

Some, some, some I, some I mur - der, some I, some I let go. _____

Some, some, some I, some I mur - der, some I, some I let go. _____

D.S. al Coda

CODA

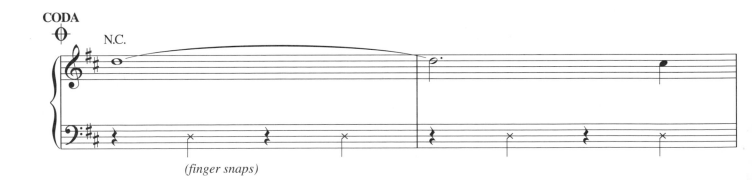

(finger snaps)

RINGA RINGA

Music by A R RAHMAN
Lyrics by RAQUIB ALAM

ring - a, ring - a ring - a ring - a, ring - a ring - a ring - a ring - a

1 ring - a. Ring - a ring - a ring - a. **2** Kha - ti - ye pe

mein pa - di thi, Aur geh - ri neend ba - di thi.

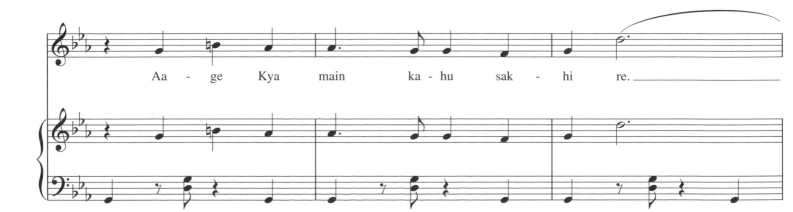

Aa - ge Kya main ka - hu sak - hi re.

ku - ch na - hi so - cha. Ren - g ke jaa -

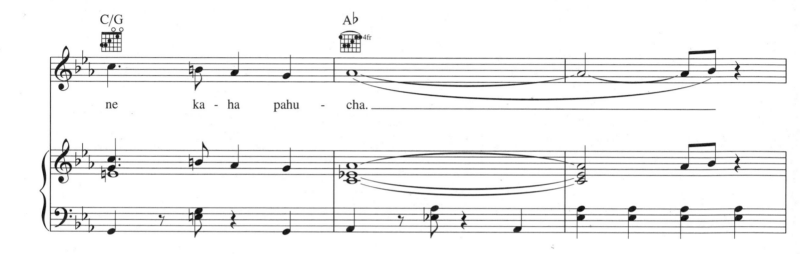

ne ka - ha pahu - cha. _____

Ring - a ring - a ring - a, ring - a ring - a

ring - a ring - a ring - a ring - a ring - a ring - a. Ring - a ring - a

Chain __ l - le - ne na di - ya. Ro - na bhi

cha - ha to muj - kho ro - ne na - di - ya. __

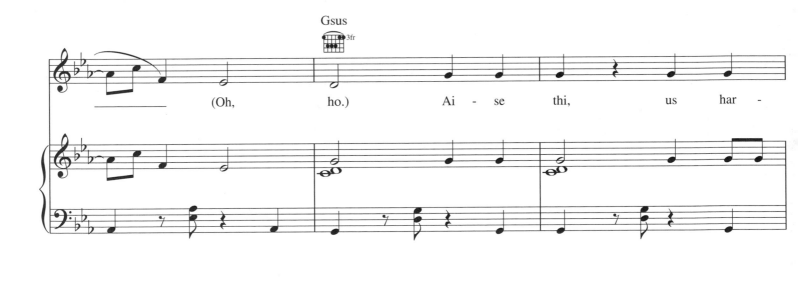

__ (Oh, ho.) Ai - se thi, us har -

ja - i ki mak - ka - ri. Me - re tan ba - dan mein

thi la - gi chin - ga - ri. Ooh,
(Spoken:) Per aise kya thi lachari.

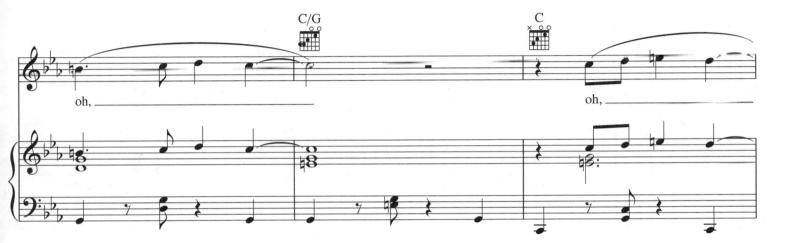

oh, _____ oh, _____

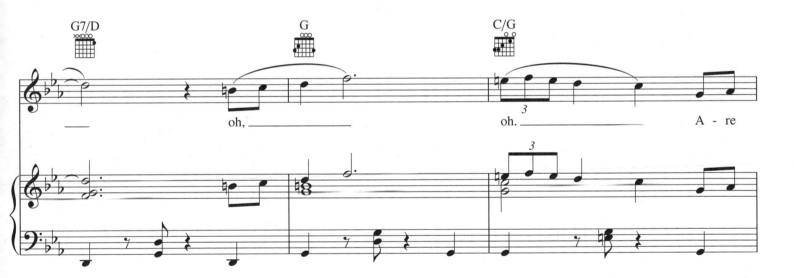

oh, _____ oh. _____ A - re

hai - ya yai - ya hoo. Ring - a ring - a ring - a, ring - a ring - a

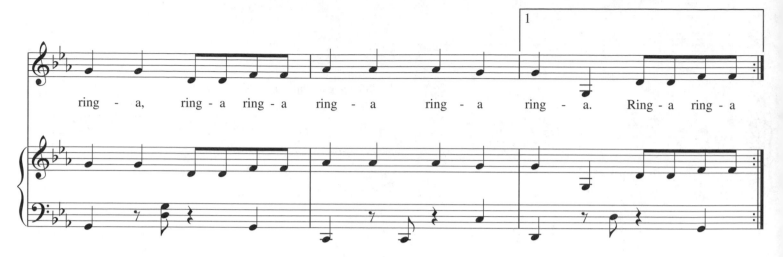

ring - a, ring - a ring - a ring - a ring - a ring - a. Ring - a ring - a

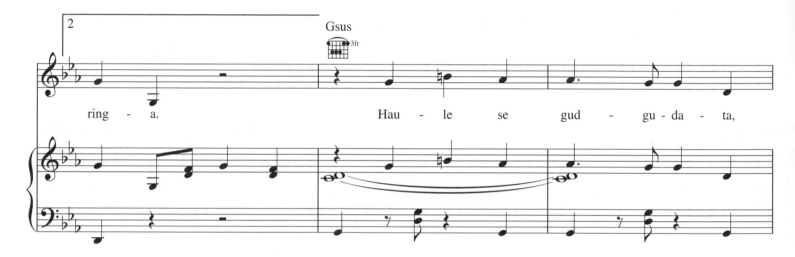

ring - a. Hau - le se gud - gu - da - ta,

dil mein hul - chul ma - cha - ta. Mein shar - ma

se thi pa - ni pa - ni. _____

Jo us-ko dhun-thi mein chup-ke se

woh chup __ ja - ta, ai - se thi woh me - ri ka -

ha - ni. Jhu khu. _____

_ Yun sam - j - lo khat-mal ka shi -

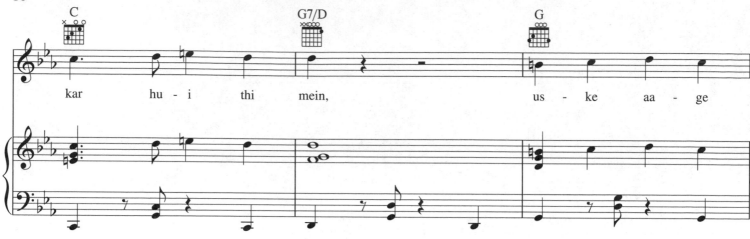

kar hu - i thi mein, us - ke aa - ge

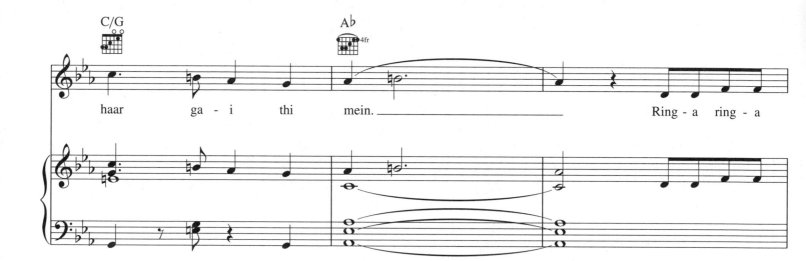

haar ga - i thi mein. _____ Ring - a ring - a

ring - a, ring - a ring - a ring - a, ring - a ring - a ring - a ring - a

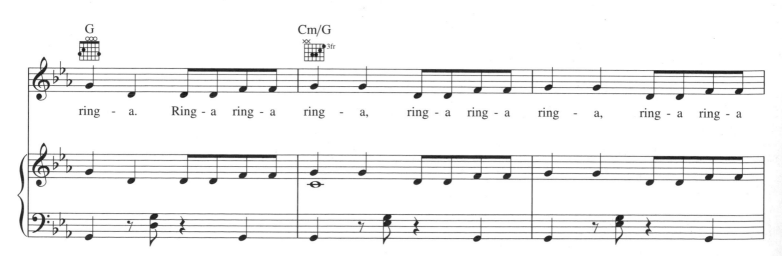

ring - a. Ring - a ring - a ring - a, ring - a ring - a ring - a, ring - a ring - a

LATIKA'S THEME

Music and Lyrics by
A R RAHMAN

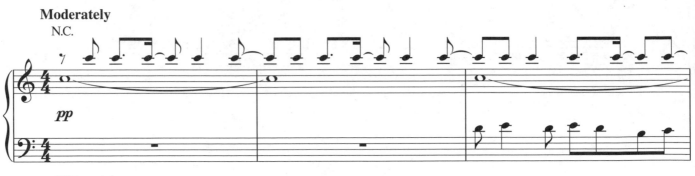

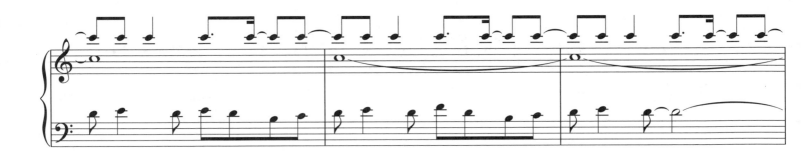

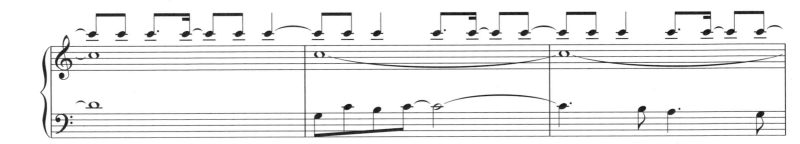

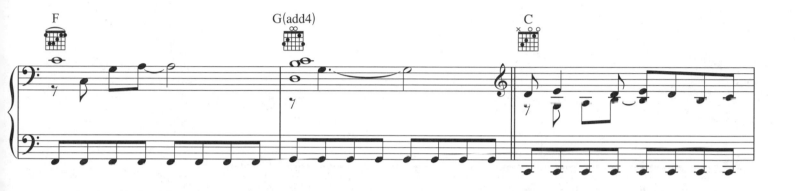

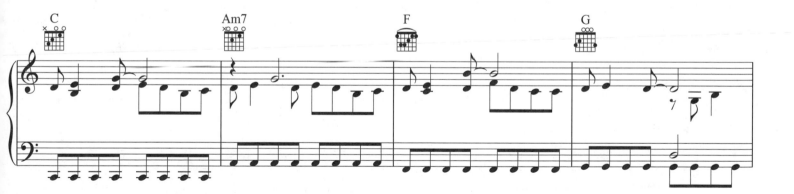

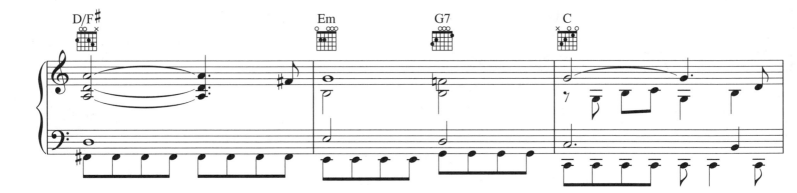

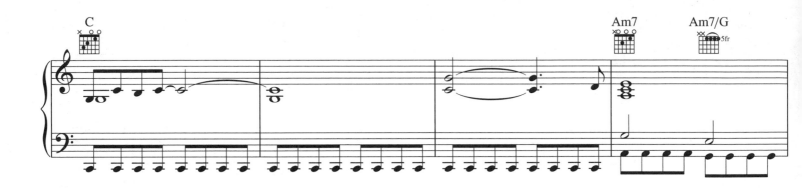

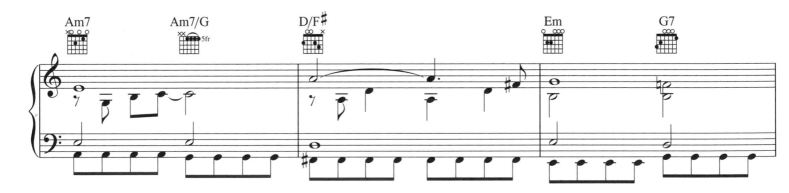

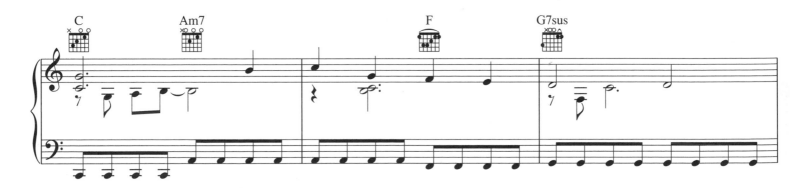

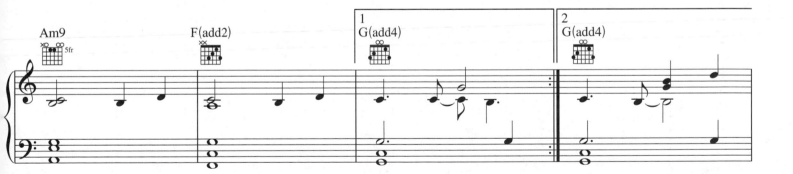

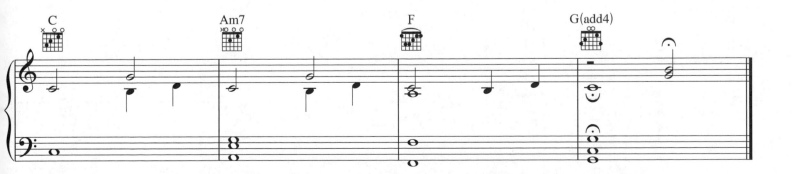

AAJ KI RAAT

Words and Music by SHANKAR MAHADEVAN,
EHSAAN NOORANI, ALOYSUIS MENDONSA
and JAVED AKHTAR

Moderately fast

Recorded a half step lower.

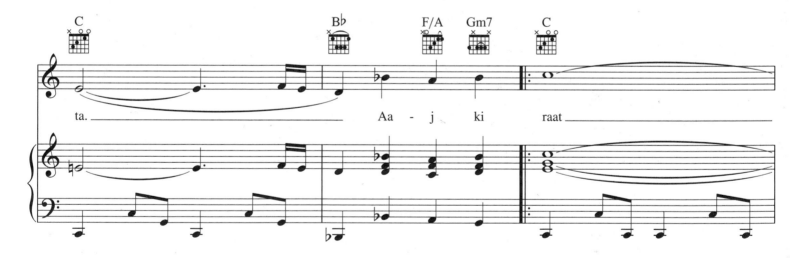

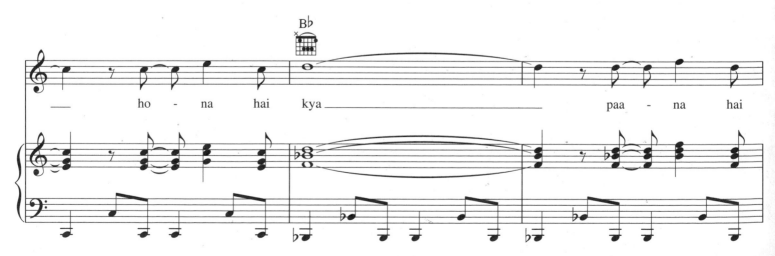

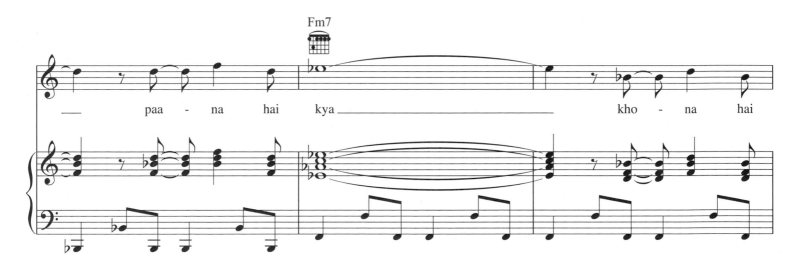

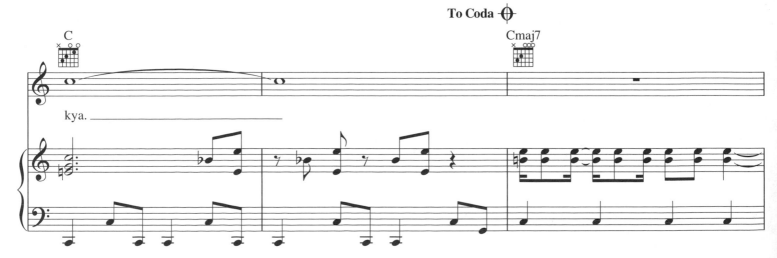

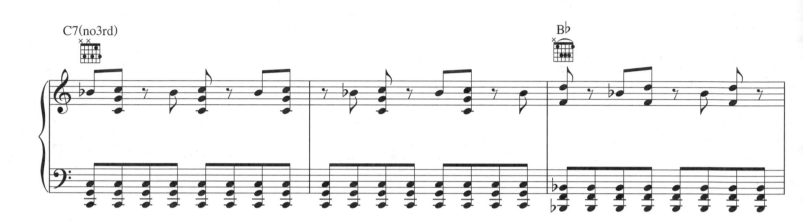

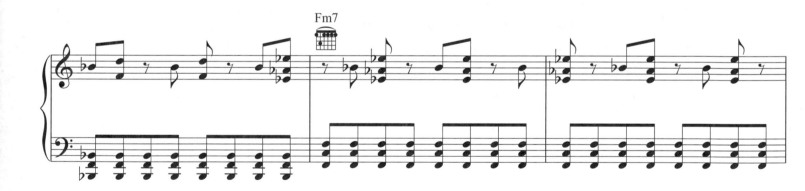

D.S. al Coda

CODA

Repeat and Fade   **Optional Ending**

MILLIONAIRE

Music and Lyrics by
A R RAHMAN

Moderately fast

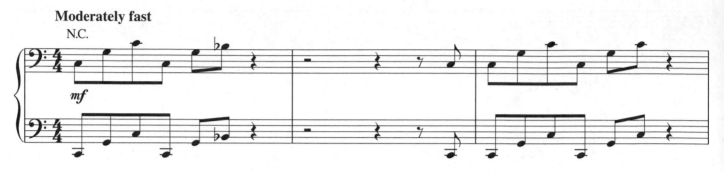

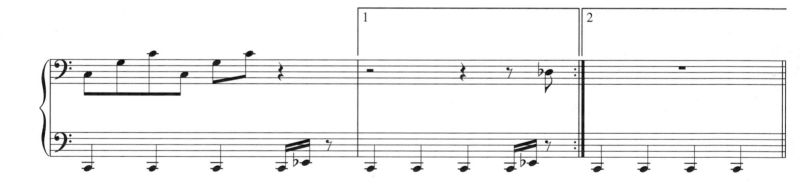

Play 3 times

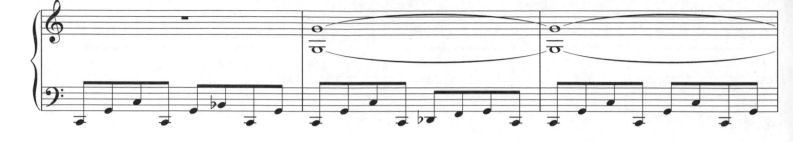

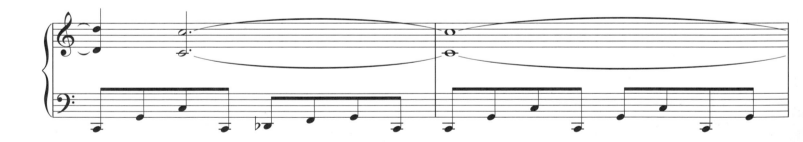

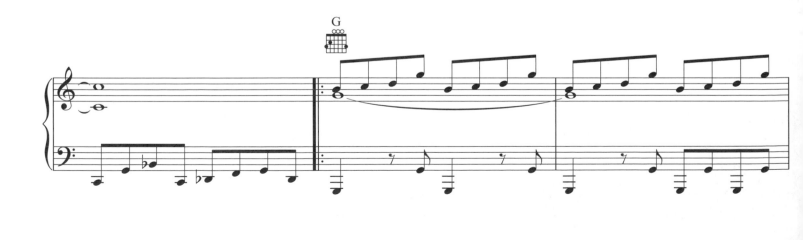

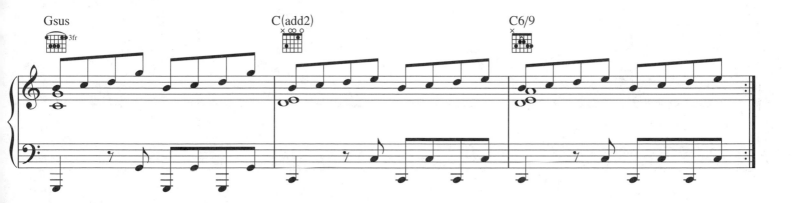

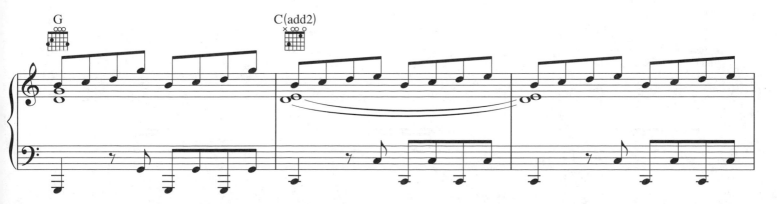

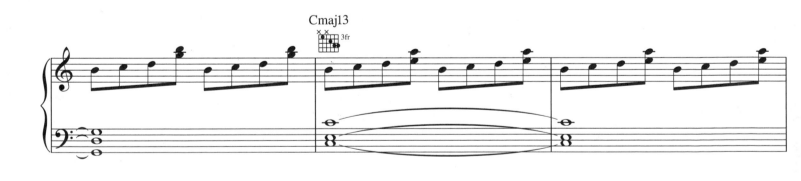

DREAMS ON FIRE

Music by A R RAHMAN
Lyrics by WENDY PAAR and BlaaZe

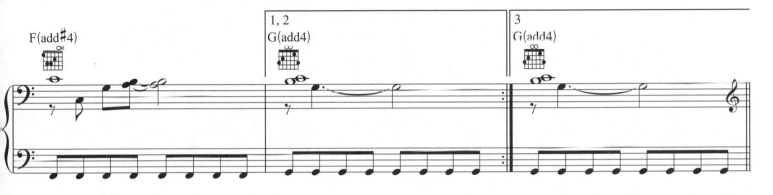

You are my wak-ing dream, __ you're all that's real to me, __
You are my o-cean waves, __ you are my thought each day, __

you are the mag-ic in the world I see. __
you are the laugh-ter from child-hood games. __

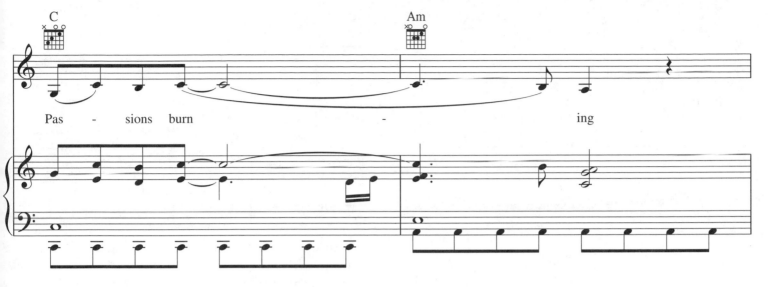

Pas - sions burn - ing

bright on the pyre. _____ One

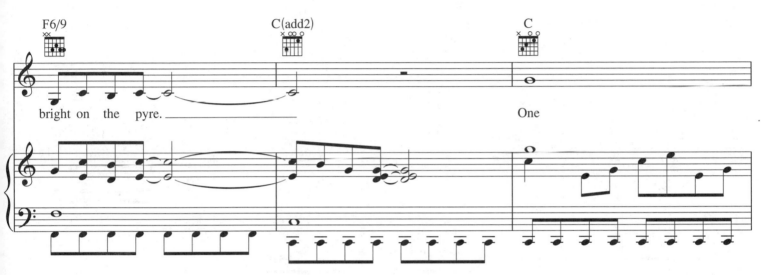

spark, for - ev - er __ yours,

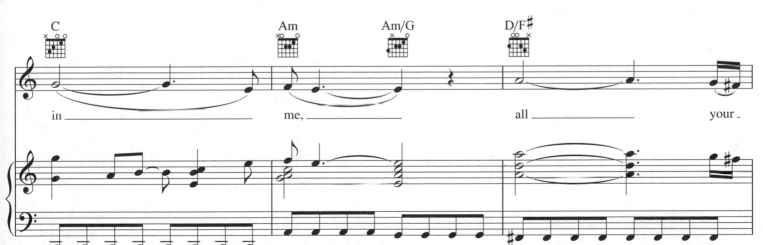

in _____ me, _____ all _____ your _

heart.   Dreams _____   on   fi -

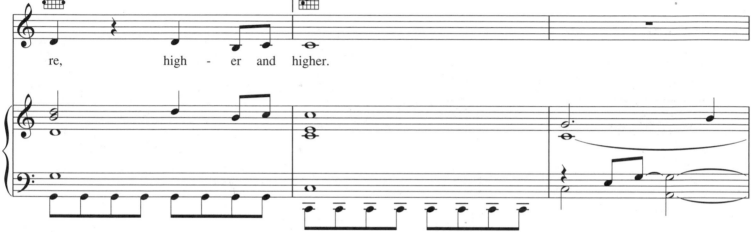

re,   high - er and higher.

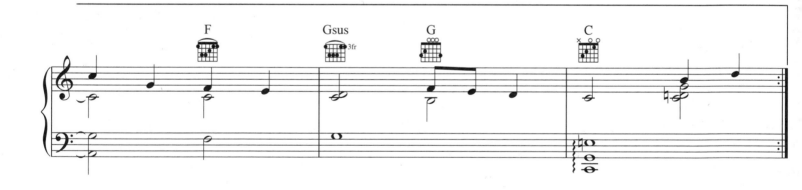

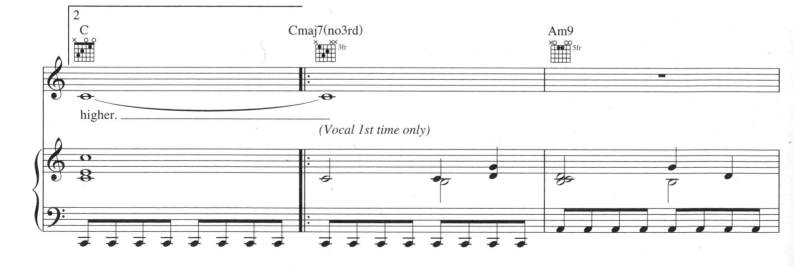

higher. _____

(Vocal 1st time only)

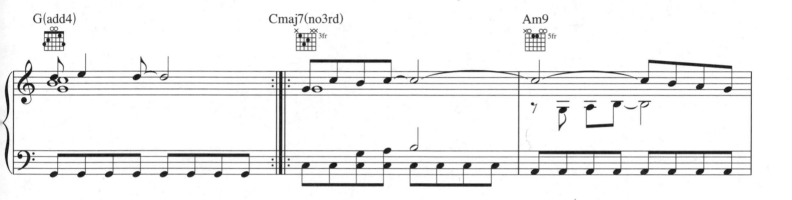

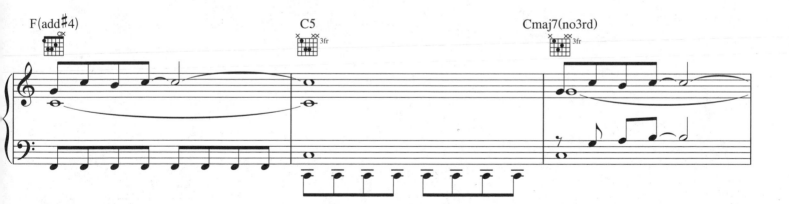

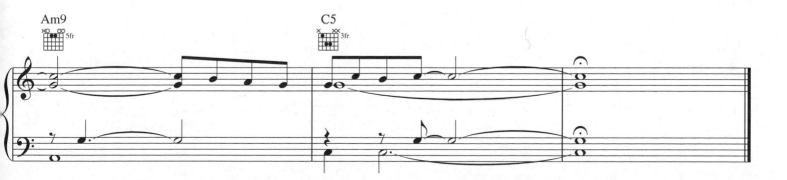

JAI HO

Music by A R RAHMAN
Lyrics by GULZAR and TANVI SHAH

(Ja - i   ho,

ja - i   ho,   ja - i

ho, ja - i ho.)

Am

Aa - ja aa - ja jin - de sha - mi - ya - ne ke ta - le, aa - ja

ja - ri - wa - le ni - le aa - su - ma - ne ke ta - le. ___ (Ja - i ho,

ja - i ho.)

Aa - ja aa - ja jin - de sha - mi - ya - ne ke ta - le, aa - ja ja - ri - wa - le ni - le aa - su -

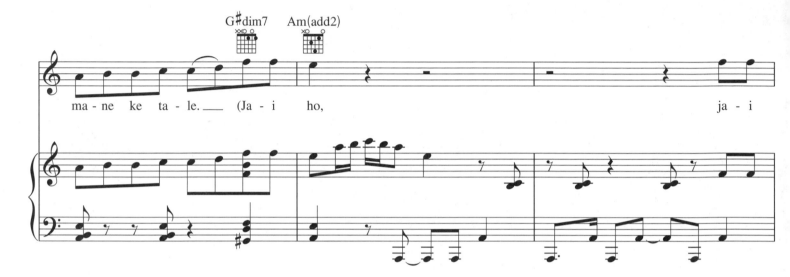

G#dim7 Am(add2)

ma - ne ke ta - le. ___ (Ja - i ho, ja - i

Cmaj7

ho.) Ja - i ho, ___

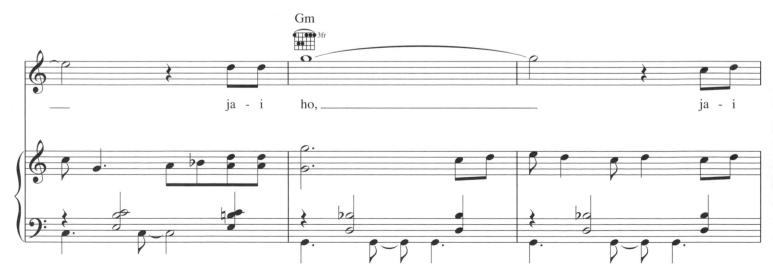

Gm

ja - i ho, ___ ja - i

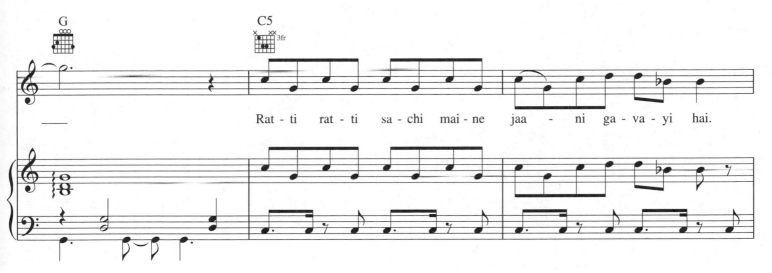

Hai aa - ja aa - ja jin - de sha - mi - ya - ne ke ta - le, aa - ja ja - ri - wa - le ni - le aa - su -

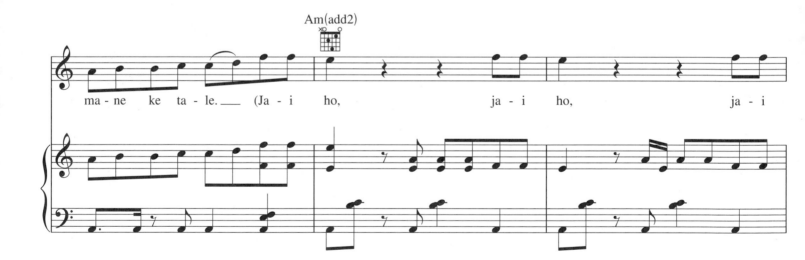

ma - ne ke ta - le. __ (Ja - i ho, ja - i ho, ja - i

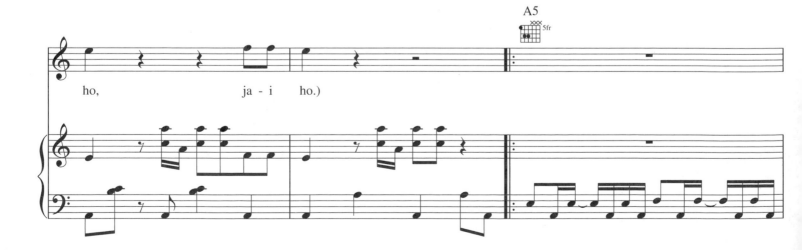

ho, ja - i ho.)

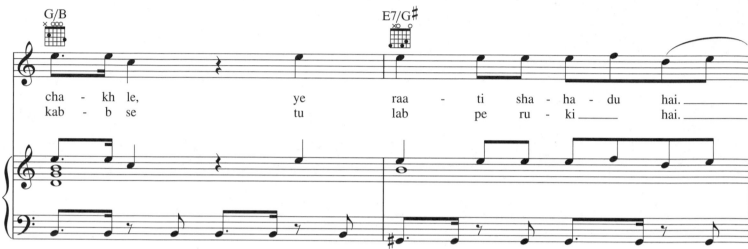

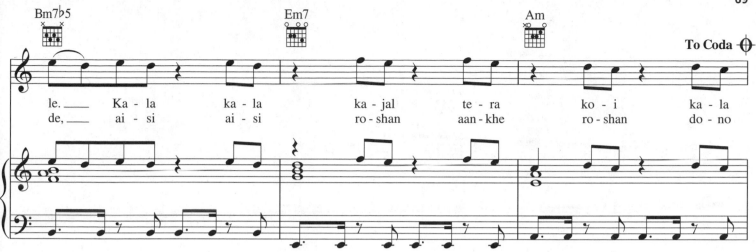

le. ___ Ka - la ka - la ka - jal te - ra ko - i ka - la
de, ___ ai - si ai - si ro - shan aan - khe ro - shan do - no

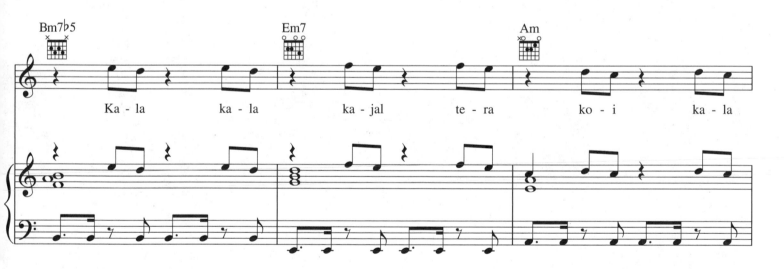

ja - doo hai na.

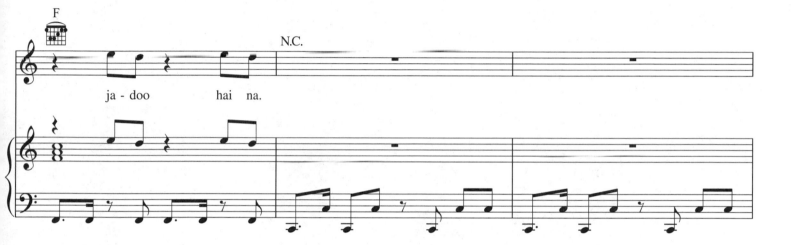

Ka - la ka - la ka - jal te - ra ko - i ka - la

ja - doo hai na. Aa - ja aa - ja jin - de sha - mi - ya - ne ke ta - le, aa - ja

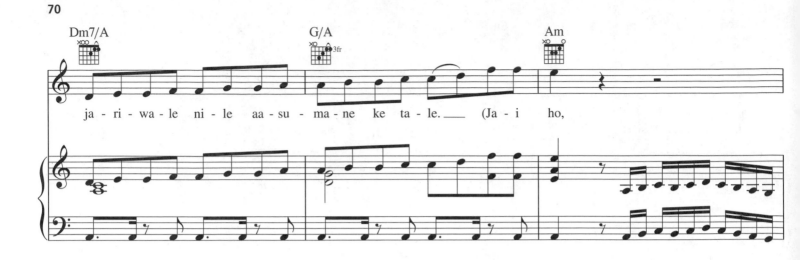

ja - ri - wa - le ni - le aa - su - ma - ne ke ta - le.____ (Ja - i ho,

ja - i ho.)

D.S. al Coda

Ja - i

CODA

bhi hai   hai kya.

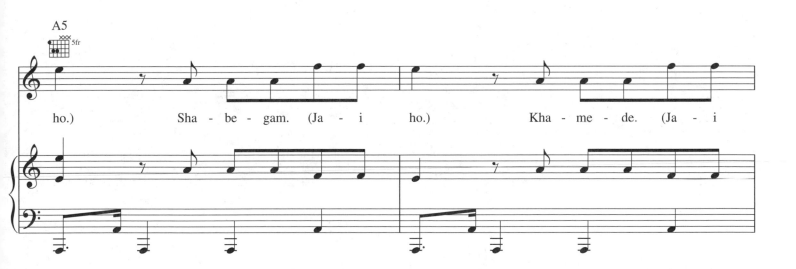

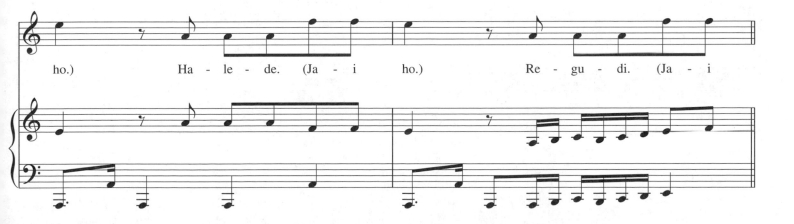

ho.) (¡Bai - la, bai - la!) (Ja - i ho.)

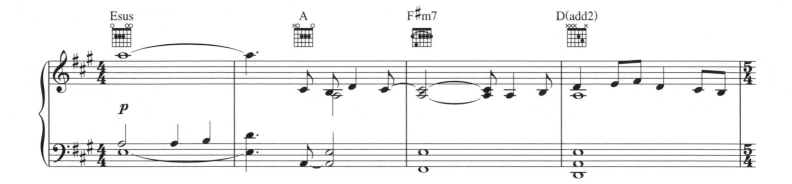

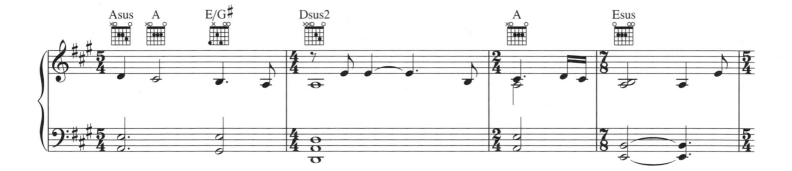

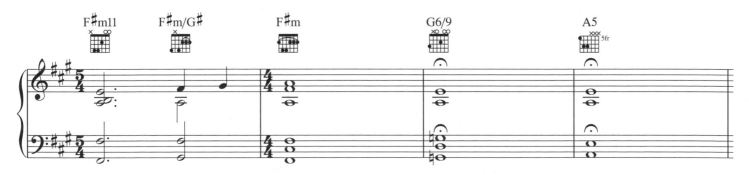

Additional Lyrics

Ahora con migo, tu baila para hoy
Por nuestro dia de movidas,
Las problemas los que sea.
¡Salud! ¡Baila, baila!